THE HILLS WE CLIMB:
LOVE IT, HATE IT,
EMBRACE IT...LIFE'S JOURNEY

Kenneth Pinckney

COPYRIGHT PAGE

THE HILLS WE CLIMB: LOVE IT, HATE IT, EMBRACE IT... LIFE'S JOURNEY

TABLE OF CONTENTS

INTRODUCING ME

The Lord directs the steps of the godly, He delights in every detail of their lives. Though they stumble, they will never fall, for the Lord holds them by the hand. (Psalms 37: 23-24, Life Application Study Bible, NLT).

For just as the heavens are higher than the earth, so my ways are higher than your ways and my thoughts higher than your thoughts. (Isaiah 55:9, Life Application Study Bible, NLT).

I had plans, but God had other ideas. My plans were to live a simple life, stay in one place, work one job, and retire quietly. Little did I know that my life would be full of twists, turns, ups-and-downs, uncertainties, valleys, and hills to climb.

If you had told me when I was growing up in a rural small town that I'd be an entrepreneur, a runner, and an adventurer with friends from around the world, I never would have believed you. But here I am!

The Hills We Climb:
Love it, Hate it, Embrace it...Life's Journey

The road here has not been an easy one. I have been on a journey to find where I belong; to find who I really am. I have stumbled -- stumbled a lot. I've been misdirected, lost, and filled with self-doubt. I've taken a lot of chances, moved to a lot of places, climbed lots of hills and fallen down quite a few of them.

Everything has been a process, and a lot of things I've tried haven't worked out. I've constantly had to adapt and adjust, but this has kept me humble; kept me from getting too high *or* too low. And all along, my Heavenly Father has kept me in His hand, guiding me to where I needed to be. I believe He had to put me through the fire of life to mold me and shape me to be where I am now. I had to fail in order to change. I had to be transformed to come out better than I was before.

It took something as simple as running to find where I needed to be; to embrace who I am. It took running to find my purpose: inspiring others. Running has helped me to embrace the journey in life, the ups and downs. To embrace the hills -- and to keep climbing.

The Hills We Climb:
Love it, Hate it, Embrace it...Life's Journey

I realized over the past few years, especially since the beginning of COVID, everyone has a story to share. A story that people could find inspiration and hope in. I am very grateful that running has given me a platform to tell my story...with the world -- not only with runners, but with everyone – to share how I embraced my purpose in life; to run up that hill and not turn back in becoming "LiveRunBoundless".

At 8,859 feet tall, Mt. Cucamonga is one of the highest peaks of the San Gabriel Mountains in California. I climbed it.

Mt. Gorgonio is 11,503 feet in elevation, making it the highest peak in Southern California. I reached the top. On the way back down, I almost needed a medical helicopter, but I continued walking on my own two feet.

The Baja Ultra 50K race in Mexico has very steep hills and a high elevation. It was a challenge. Crossing beautiful rivers and creeks was somewhat fun -- and hot.

The Hills We Climb:
Love it, Hate it, Embrace it...Life's Journey

I attempted this race but did not finish (DNF). I was broken and hurt. A piece of my soul was left behind.

Just recently, I ran a relay trail race I had not planned on doing. I did not know the trail well. I got lost in the dark. Eight miles turned into more like 16 miles, but I was able to find my way back. You know what? I am willing to go back and do it again. It also took me 50 times to pass my Navy swim qualification.

This is my journey, this is my hill, this is my story.

CHAPTER ONE

Hemingway, South Carolina

The journey from where I began to where I am now has been full of twists, turns, and ups and downs—more downs than ups, it seemed at times. If I'm going to explain the journey of my life, I have to go back to a small town in South Carolina where I was born and raised called Hemingway.

The population of Hemingway was 459 according to the 2010 census and 522 according to the 2020 census, so the town is growing. But it's still smaller now than it was when I was born in 1976, when it had a population of 1,026.

If you happen to know anything about my town, it's probably because you passed it on the way to Myrtle Beach, or you stopped in to eat at our famous Rodney Scott's Barbeque. After all, the Hemingway, SC website does say the town is the "Barbecue Capital of the World." But barbecue isn't all we have to offer; you cannot go through Hemingway without visiting Fish Net Seafood Diner. Our one other claim to fame is the Tupperware manufacturing plant. Other than that, this is still a rural farming community, with tobacco as the main crop.

Life in Hemingway, South Carolina

At age seventeen, I was more than ready to leave my hometown, but I have also learned over the years to appreciate where I came from and not take it for granted. The simple life of a small town was not always easy, yet I appreciate my family and the surrounding community.

The Hemingway area is made up of small cities and communities. I think a good place to start is Brunson Crossroad. Why Brunson Crossroad? Because it's home to the world-famous Scott's Barbeque, now Rodney Scott Barbeque, is named after its renowned chef. The restaurant has been around since the 1970's. You cannot come to Hemingway without stopping by to get some pit pulled pork BBQ, some Red n' Rock soda, and maybe even some chocolate cake.

Then there's Stuckey, SC. about four miles from Hemingway with a population of 245. What is Stuckey known for? Well, the one-and-only Nesmith & Pinckney funeral home, which was founded sixty-two years ago by my great-grandfather, York Carver Pinckney, and Mr. Eddie Nesmith, and is still going strong, serving the community. Another memorable place from the past that may still be around today is the Stuckey laundromat.

Going to Stuckey laundromat on a Friday night was the thing for us to do for a while. Before we had our own washing machine, every Friday night on which my mother didn't have to work overtime, my sister and I used to go there with her to wash clothes. This was where I'd see friends or other kids in the community, and we'd play basketball on the laundromat's basketball court if the other fellas would let me.

Then you had Bubba Tanner's Grocery, which was a staple in the Stuckey community, and outside as well. It was a family-run grocery store where we could shop for a full cart of groceries for twenty dollars, talk to friends and neighbors, and just have a grand old time. I have lots of great memories of Bubba Tanner's; it's sad that it's closed down now.

Down the road a little bit from Stuckey, you have Nesmith, SC. I never really spent time in Nesmith. I had, and still have, family members there but like I say, "we all cousins." Nesmith is best known for its school, Battery Park. This school has a long history. Both of my parents graduated from high school there, when it went up to the 12th grade. By the time I arrived at Battery, there was no longer a high school; the school went up to 8th grade, and after that, the majority of the kids went to Hemingway High School in town.

The main thing that stood out about the Battery Park school was that the majority of kids were Black. I didn't mix in with white kids until I went to Hemingway High.

The Hills We Climb:
Love it, Hate it, Embrace it...Life's Journey

It was not hard for me to adapt and adjust to going to school with white kids and there were never really any issues. Some of my favorite teachers at Battery Park were white, including Ms. Allen and my Basketball Coach/P.E. teacher, Mr. Altman.

Past Nesmith, you have another community called St. Mark, mostly because St. Mark African Methodist Episcopal Church is located there. When I was young, most people in the community attended St. Mark. I could call it the Mega Church of Hemingway but it is so much more. St. Mark church is a church of long history dating back to my great grandparents. St. Mark is a church where I was raised, going to Sunday School, saying my bible verses, "The Lord is my Shepard, I shall not want". My fondest memory of growing up in the church, were the two or what seemed like three-hour church services and the memories of taking a nap on mom's lap when the pastor was preaching. That was the best. Another memory was being in the back of the church playing with friends and goofing off.

As I got older, I had to usher and sing in the choir. I believe every kid sang in the choir even if they didn't know how to sing, which I didn't mind. I enjoyed hanging out with the rest of the kids. St. Mark church was a community, when someone left home and come back to visit, they always have to come back to St. Mark to visit. No matter how far you go, you are always a part of St. Mark. We are all family.

Also in the St. Mark community was Cooper Grocery, or Cooper Store. This was a family-owned, Black-owned store. It wasn't just a place to shop; it was a place where people came to hang out, mess around, drink soda pop or alcohol, and have some snacks. Again, everyone knew one another, and everyone was family. At nighttime, it turned into a club or juke joint where people got their party on grown folks and kids as well. Picture that.

If you were hungry, a lady named Ms. Boy (I never did know how she got her nickname, but that's what everyone called her) as the mom of the store. She did the cooking and served up some simple Southern food, like some good ol' Chicken Perlo or Chicken and Rice cooked together served with a slice of white bread on the side, a side of greens, and sometimes BBQ. It was nothing fancy, but it was really good.

Growing up in Hemingway

My family lived in a rural area of Hemingway, about twenty miles from the city limit. Life growing up there was simple, but not always easy and not always fun.

As an adult, especially now at my age, and after all I've experienced, I appreciate getting up early in the morning so I can have my "me time," where I can focus, pray, read, or run for a while before I get out into the world. As a kid, I dreaded waking up early in the morning, with my dad coming into my bedroom before the crack of dawn, turning on the lights, and telling me and my sister to wake up. I was just not feeling it. Growing up, early mornings meant going to work with my dad to his job at the restaurant (one of many he worked at over the years) at times, feeding the pigs before I went to school, or working in our big garden. It wasn't the kind of garden you see in the city, but the kind where you need a tractor to plow the long rows in the field. We grew rows of tomatoes, cabbage, collard greens, string beans, snap peas, squash, okra, watermelon and many other veggies.

Not only did I work the family garden, but my first summer job was working in the tobacco field. For three summers, I had to crop tobacco for $20 a day, which is not much today, but for a kid in the early '90s, it was huge. Working in any type of field was hard. I did try getting a job working at the beach, like a hotel, restaurant, grocery store, or amusement park, but I never got a call, probably because I was having too much fun hanging out with my friends on the beach and goofing off to take my job search seriously. Fun had a price—all of us ended up working in the tobacco field.

My childhood and teen years were somewhat average. I did just well enough in school to keep from failing. I always had the fear of failing and being held back or repeating another grade. There were times in high school where I struggled with my grades but somehow, I passed, doing just enough to survive and advance to the next grade. Or maybe the teachers just passed me because I was nice and likeable. That was the majority of my young life, trying to survive, to find a way to make it through in the world.

I had childhood friends and a big family with lots of cousins. Really, when you come from a small town, everyone is a cousin. Family was important, and family reunions were a must growing up in Hemingway. Fortunately for me, I had two family reunions to go to on my dad's side of the family. My dad was adopted, so we had his adoptive family, the Pinckney's, and his biological family, the Dozier's and Browns. They each have family reunions about every year.

The fondest memory I have of our family is the year we had the Pinckney and the Dozier and Brown reunions on the same day. That was so much fun. We went to the Pinckney's first, then the Dozier's and Brown's family.

So yes, the family was big, and we were all related in some type of way. Every time I go home to visit, there are so many people and family members to see and spend time with. Sometimes there's not enough time to visit everyone.

I've always had a roof over my head, food to eat (and I mean plenty to eat) at home, at Grandma's house, at my other grandma's house, at all my aunties' houses, at other family members' houses, and even at strangers' houses.

Another thing that stands out in my memory about growing up in Hemingway is going down the rugged dirt roads; the kind that throw your tires out of whack and only allow you to drive ten miles per hour most of the time. Sometimes it would take forever to get to someone's house because of the bumps, ditches, and rocky terrain. There were some dirt roads you just didn't want to drive down at night because they cut through dark, lonely woods, and there was always the fear someone would come out of nowhere and attack. That would never really happen, but your mind plays games with you out there. Then there were the narrow dirt roads, where you had to pull off to the side if another car came toward you going in the opposite direction. That's how bad some of those roads were. Some probably still are that bad.

Hemingway was a rural area, and we always enjoyed going out to bigger towns and seeing the city lights. Going to Wal Mart was a big thing for us. We'd get cleaned up and dressed up to go there. At that time, there was only one Wal Mart close to Hemingway, and it was twenty miles away. Wal Mart was my mom's favorite place to go to because she was a seamstress and she enjoyed looking at their patterns and sewing materials. I *always* had to wait on her until she was done.

We enjoyed going out to eat at Wendy's. The fast-food restaurant was really a special treat; the burger looked so good on TV, and was delicious in real life.

At one time, I took those small moments in life for granted, but now I'm grateful for them. I'm also grateful for later opportunities to go out and explore, and all of the special moments I experienced outside of the place where I was born and raised.

One thing about living in a small town: we tried to keep everything in-house. We did have issues just like everyone else. We didn't talk about them or seek a lot of outside counsel for our problems. Things were very simple; you were either a good kid or a bad kid, a good person or bad person, no in-between. We never considered mental health or trauma. Maybe we weren't educated on those things in the '80s and '90s like we are today.

I grew up in a four-person home: Dad, Mom, my older sister, and me. As I've mentioned, outside of our immediate family, I had lots of uncles, aunts, grandparents I spent time with.

I adored my Granddad Pinckney. He passed away too soon, when I was only around ten years of age. I believe my life could have been much different if he had lived another five or ten years. I would have loved to have spent more time with him; I could have learned so much more from being around him. Maybe I would have made fewer mistakes in life. I can still remember him taking my sister and me around on the tractor as he plowed the fields or taking us for rides in his pick-up truck. We would bounce around in the back on the truck bed as we went down to the old country store.

I only had one grandfather, and only for a little while. But I was blessed to have three grandmothers and two great grandmothers. Grandmother Pinckney passed away a year after Granddad Pinckney. For as long as I could remember, she'd been sick. I remember walking very slowly by her side and watching her hands as they shook badly from Parkinson's Disease. She eventually became bedridden and unable to do anything for herself. Even her food had to be cut up into small pieces and fed to her. The one memory that stands out most to me about Grandmother Pinckney was having the privilege of feeding her breakfast. It was such a simple act, but the heart behind it made it so special.

Grandma Minnie, or Ma, as I called her, was also special to me. She was my mother's mom and on many a summer day, my mom would drop my sister and me off at Ma's house—a lime sorbet-green single-wide trailer -- while my mom went to work. I have many great memories of being there.

Sometimes, my mom's youngest sister would drop off her five kids at Ma's house also. It was so much fun, hanging out the whole day with one another. Ma had a basketball hoop in the backyard, and my cousin Junior and I would play basketball almost the whole day. Ma's brother and sister-in-law and their kids lived next door to her. They had their own basketball court also, and sometimes we'd go to their house and play basketball

all day. No matter how hot it was, we enjoyed playing outside and being free.

As a kid, I learned to stay out of grown folks' conversations. As I got older, I would have grown-up conversations with my Ma, and I realized that I had finally arrived!

What I liked most about being at my Grandma Minnie's house, once again, was the food. It wasn't anything fancy, but it was really good. Ma used to cook some homemade biscuits and sweet breads. Sometimes she'd serve the sweet bread with cooked blueberries with juice coming out of them; so sweet and delicious. I used to dip the sweet bread into the bowl of blueberries, and it was food heaven. She would also make dishes like chicken and rice cooked together with salt and pepper. Very simple dishes, but when she made them, they came out delicious.

As much as I enjoyed the food my grandma cooked, I know it was not healthy for me. I saw the impact it had on Ma's life. One of my lasting memories of my

The Hills We Climb:
Love it, Hate it, Embrace it...Life's Journey

Grandma Minnie is when I came to visit her as an adult and both of her legs had been amputated due to complications from diabetes and lack of self-care. She was bedridden, and my uncle and aunt had to take care of her around the clock. It was tough to see someone who used to take care of us need constant care.

I was away on a ship serving in the Navy when she died. Due to my grandmother not being an immediate relative, I was not able to go home to be with the family. I remember when I was on the ship and I got the phone call from my mother through Red Cross because I was deployed. My mother told me the news of my grandmother's passing. Little did I know that a year later, after dealing with some health issues herself, my mother would pass away as well.

It's hard to put into words how much I miss my mother and grandmother.

***

Then there was Grandma Sally, my dad's birth mom. I loved me some Grandma Sally, and she loved me. She always called me Kennedy. I never really knew why. I figured she just liked the name. I have so much gratitude for having the opportunity to know my dad's birth family and to have known and been around my Grandma Sally.

I enjoyed my time being at her house, and of course, the food she cooked. She was known for her Hoppin' John: black-eyed peas and rice with some flavored pork meat, like ham hock or fatback to go with it. Again, something so simple but oh-so-good. What I really enjoyed and miss the most is my grandmother Sally's world-renowned fruitcake, made from scratch. Almost every Christmas, I could count on my grandmother's fruit cake. I know people give it a bad rap, but I love fruitcake! More specifically Grandma Sally's fruitcake. She put *all* the ingredients in it, the nuts, the green cherries, the red cherries, maybe some blue cherries, who knows? It always came out dark, moist, and tasted good with soda pop or milk. Grandmother Sally always made sure I had a piece or two, even when she was away for the Christmas holidays. She knew that I wanted her fruit cake.

She was doing all that cooking and baking in spite of her own health issues: arthritis, bad knees, and other things I probably didn't know about. Grandmother Sally had her challenges in life. She had to give up her kids, including my dad, but seeing that she still loved them, and loved us, gave me so much gratitude and love for all my family.

My relationship with my family -- well, I did love them, but things weren't always the best, especially with my dad and sister.

That journey of my life, we will get to in later chapters.

CHAPTER TWO

The Growing Pains of Love for My Dad

I believe you can take some good and bad from any relationship. That was definitely the case with my dad and sister. I have to start with my dad. He was, or is, the main reason I started my journey to seek something better, and the reason I had this desire to keep pushing forward, climbing that hill of life, and not turning back, not going back.

I believe my dad did the best he could in the way he raised my sister and me. There was just one aspect of his personality or his character that instilled fear into me and made me unable to really express myself. He wanted everything done just so, and if I didn't do it right, I knew what was coming and it wasn't good. We did not have the laughing, joking, friendly, touchy, hugging kind of relationship. Other than sports, we had very little in common, and even then, we liked totally opposite teams — him, the Boston Celtics and me, the Lakers.

Looking back, sports were probably the biggest thing I appreciate about having my father for a dad, especially enjoying the game of baseball as an adult. I did not enjoy it as a kid. I remember those hot, muggy summer days and nights in the South. My dad would turn off the TV and turn on the radio, sit on the porch in the rocking chair, and listen to the Atlanta Braves. This was in the 80s, before they became really good in the '90s with a list of All-Star pitchers. That's when I jumped on the Braves bandwagon! Listening to baseball on the radio was the most boring thing ever, I thought. That was my dad, Mr. Old-School.

My father and I both like to cook. And my dad was part of gospel quartet group, and I really like music and enjoy singing, but that was where our similarities ended.

The Hills We Climb:
Love it, Hate it, Embrace it...Life's Journey

My dad really was old-school in all his way of thinking — very traditional. Which is not always bad. I just did not agree with his ways of doing some things. Unfortunately, if I didn't do things a certain way—or his way, the look on his face would frighten me, or the raising of his hands. Raised hands were soon followed by the belt or the broom. I am not saying he was abusive or that anyone needed to call Child Welfare Services, but it was not relaxing being around him.

I remember during my grandmother's funeral, when I was very emotional and crying, my dad told me, "No crying! No crying!" I didn't even get a hug from him, nor did he tell me everything would be okay.

Maybe one good thing I can say came from my relationship with my dad is that I learned to behave like a man and not like a girl. That's how it was for me growing up. I did my best to please my dad, but there was no pleasing him. If my dad was like my granddad or other men I knew in the community who took me under their wing and took the time to teach me things without yelling, maybe it would been a little bit easier to spend time with him, and maybe I would have wanted to be around him more. Instead, I preferred to spend time with my mom. My best memories of living at home were those days when my dad was away for the weekend or going to the VA doctor for regular check-ups in Charleston, S.C., an hour and a half away.

One more thing I could say I gained from my relationship with my dad was learning to wake up early in the morning. As a kid, I used to hate it when he woke us up — he'd turn on the light, sometimes before the crack of dawn, for what to me seemed like random reasons. Sometimes there were real reasons, like feeding the pigs, working in the garden, or my sister having to make breakfast, or doing household chores. But other times, it was just my dad being who he was. Even though it is a struggle getting up at 4 or 5 in the mornings, it is so worth it. I need that time of stillness, mediating on God's Word and maybe going for an early morning run to get my day started.

Sometimes we had to go to work with my dad early in the morning at one of the restaurants where he was a cook. Those were mornings I really did not enjoy; doing hard jobs with him in a hot kitchen, sometimes for no money, was not fun, it was brutal. He was always yelling. We never could do anything right. Once, when he took us to work with him, he wanted us to do something a certain way, but my sister and I could not get it right. My dad got frustrated, took a broomstick and started beating us on the behind. Things had to be done correctly or perfectly, no mistakes, or else.

Being around my dad was truly miserable most of the time. I never felt peace or calm around him. I was always anxious and unable to be myself or express myself. I felt like I had to be perfect in everything I did. If I made a mistake or something was not done right, there was no discussion. He was quick to take out the belt.

Learning how to drive with my dad in the passenger seat was the worst. If I made one mistake or drove over a pothole or rough patch on the road, my dad was quick to yell, raise his hand and put fear into me. I never understand why my dad demanded so much perfection from us. He did serve in the Army; whether that could be his excuse, I never really did know.

I don't consider myself to have been a bad kid, or a kid who got in trouble a lot. My dad just did not have patience with us. Putting this down in words, even as a 45-year-old man, is tough and very emotional for me.

Even as an adult, I could not be myself or express myself around my dad — that fear was still there. I used to dread coming home to visit him. Once my mother and dad separated and I was on my own, I preferred spending time with my mom. But, as I felt I needed to be a good son, I obligated myself to spend time with my father, too, driving him to this place and that place, and doing things for him that I shouldn't have because they probably were not right.

Of all the times I was upset with my father, there are two that stand out to me as the toughest. One was the loss of Grandfather and Grandmother Pinckney's house. The house was already paid for. After they passed away, the house belonged to us, and my parents refinanced it. Over time, it was harder and harder to make the payments.

Eventually, I moved away. I was living and working in Charlotte, N.C. when I got a call from my mom that they were about to lose the house because they couldn't make a payment. Then my dad called me and told me to see if I could come up with the money. I was so upset over the whole situation that I came home one more time to console my mother and my sister. My dad was not around.

I was hurt and upset to see this house that I had kind of grown up in, and where I'd spent time with my Granddad and Grandmother Pinckney, taken away. And yes, I blame my father for letting that happen, and putting it on me to get money to save the house. Unfortunately, I was not able to do it. That was a tough moment.

The other tough moment was when my mother passed away after battling colon cancer for several years. I was 36 years old and living in San Diego at the time. A week before she passed away, I was able to travel to South Carolina to spend time with her, but that almost didn't happen because my father said I didn't need to come. Fortunately, thanks to another family member, he changed his mind.

My time and heart were focused on my mother the whole week I was there. I did not go to visit my dad. After she passed away, I decided to go visit him. I had never gathered the nerve to talk back or yell at my dad until that moment. I don't remember the discussion, but I did not want to hear what my dad had to say. My heart was with my mom. Thank goodness for my dad's caregiver, who calmed both of us down. I really didn't care about how loud or disruptive I was being at that moment, though. My dad hit a nerve that hadn't been hit before. That was the first and probably the only time I ever yelled at my dad.

The Hills We Climb:
Love it, Hate it, Embrace it...Life's Journey

Maybe growing up around him was what motivated me to keep moving forward in life and not to look back or go back home, even when life got tough. Or when I didn't have any money, or when I felt lost because I was not working. There were times when my dad called me and told me to come back home, and I couldn't do it. I needed to find a way to make it through those hard times without my family—mostly my dad.

After leaving, I realized there were more opportunities in front of me than there were back home. In the end, I realized my dad was who he was, and he was not going to change. Yes, he loved me, but it was probably tough love. That was his character, and I learned to love him and to be understanding and do my best to let go of the past. But it was not easy, and still isn't, especially when I spend time reflecting on it.

I was eager to spread my wings and leave the nest when my senior year of high school came to an end, but my options were few. I was not able to go to any colleges that I applied to due to my low grades. I was also not able to join the Marines due to a twisted spine (scoliosis). That particular setback broke my heart. I shed some tears coming back from the U.S. Military Entrance Processing Command. I did not try any other branches of service, but my Heavenly Father had a plan. I do often think back and wonder, what if I had tried joining the Navy or any other branches of the military at age 18? I would have truly been the drunken sailor and that probably would not have turned out well.

When the Marines didn't work out, I tried out some different colleges, but my options were very limited in that respect. My grades were unimpressive--just good enough to graduate. I realized at this rate, I'd be back working in the tobacco field for another summer. I really did not want to go back to that life. I just could not stay home with my parents again — specifically, with my dad.

But thanks to my Heavenly Father and my community of family and friends, an opportunity came to me. On that day, my dad and I were sitting on the porch in the rocking chairs, just chilling out, and an old friend of the family showed up. He was a local pastor in the community, who we called Rev. He was a talker just like most preachers, or at least most Southern Black preachers. He had come by to tell my dad and me about a small electronics/truck driver school in Charleston, S.C. I remember it all so well, even though it was over 20 years ago.

My dad looked at me and said it was my decision to make; my call. I didn't care what type of school it was; I was ready to leave home and explore a new life. Actually, I was beyond ready. I was desperate to leave and get out from under the same roof as my dad. I wanted freedom to fly, to explore, to be me. So of course, I said yes!

It was a no-brainer. I was quickly all in — anything to get away from home; to fly away. I was desperate. That process, that journey--that was what I needed.

My dad passed away on December 2, 2014. As I reflect on the journey with my dad, I had to learn how to forgive and move forward. I also had to learn how to love even when it is hard to love. Maybe we didn't have the best relationship as Father and son, maybe that just the path I had to take in this life to become the person I needed to be.

The Growing Pains of Love for My Sister

For me, the ability to forgive and love someone over and over again takes a lot of prayer and a spiritual heart and mindset. There are going to be ups and downs, hurt and pain. That's life, I guess. Just like with my dad, my relationship with my sister was not the best — and that is putting it lightly. But I have learned some lessons along the way, and I continue to learn some others.

Growing up with my sister meant a lot of drama at times, especially when we were left alone. No one really knew how afraid I was of her. Brothers and sisters get into fights all the time, but it was different with my sister. Our fights went to extremes, to the point where I was afraid if I did or said the wrong thing, my sister would attack me. I didn't know how to defend myself as a kid. I did not have a vindictive or fighting mindset; maybe because she was older and bigger than me.

One of the fights I most remember was over the simplest thing: a radio. We were just listening to our little 80s boom box, and I wanted to turn to a different radio station. All of the sudden, she flipped out and started beating me up all because she wanted her way! I could not believe it, and I truly was afraid. Another vivid memory I have is of being in the front yard, laying on the ground with my sister sitting on my chest. I know she was upset but can't remember the reason why. It was not a good situation to be in.

Even as an adult, she continued this same pattern. Once, when I was living in Charlotte, my sister drove up to visit me. Allowing her to do that was probably a big mistake, but little did I know what was going to happen. She let me drive her car, then something happened to the car that was outside of my control. It was nothing that I did, but my sister didn't understand that, and again she flipped out on me. She started attacking me in the parking lot of my apartment complex, all while holding her baby daughter. My roommates witnessed the whole thing. I could have fought back, yes, but since I had decided to make a spiritual change in my life a few months earlier, I chose not to do it. What had been a pleasant visit from my sister turned into me thinking, "I can't wait for my sister to go back home" so I could find peace.

There have been times where I've wanted to put my sister in a headlock, yes! To beat her up; to get back at her for what she did to me and the heartache she caused my mom. There was one moment when I went back to visit my family and my sister was acting up, and I decided to wrestle her down. I have to admit I enjoyed it that one time.

Even when I wasn't around my sister, I endured verbal abuse from her for years. When she got upset, she would call me and curse me out, leaving voice and text messages that were hurtful, and really an inexcusable disgrace. I had to block her number numerous times. I've often told my wife and close friends that the only person who can really get to me and get me upset is my sister. And I am a person who really doesn't get upset or yell unless I'm running up some beat-me-down hills!

As my sister and I got older and I went out on my own, my mother got the brunt of my sister's wrath. It breaks my heart every time to think about everything my mom went through with my sister, all for the sake of her grandkids.

Once, I went to visit my mom and she and I went to the Piggly Wiggly, where everyone knew everyone. My sister was having one of her moments. She followed us to the supermarket and started going off on my mom and me in the middle of the bread aisle. She verbally attacked us, yelling, calling us names that I can't and won't repeat, in front of everyone. It was shameful, but I had to let it go. That was life for our family.

Even when my mom got sick, the pattern continued. For a while, my sister did not believe that my mom was truly sick and continued to give her a hard time. At the end of my mother's life, my sister finally understood the seriousness. My mother forgave her for all the troubles and heartaches that she'd had to endure.

For a while, I blamed my sister for my mother's sickness getting worse, and for passing away so soon. I believe there is so much a person can take, and my mom took a lot from my sister, mostly for the sake of her grandkids, who she didn't want to lose. She forgave like a mom forgives, out of love for her daughter, despite what her daughter had done, and to let go and find peace before she passed away. Writing this now hits me to the heart.

Even my wife experienced the wrath of my sister once. It was something I never thought could happen, but it did. We were visiting, staying at my sister's place, and one day something happened that caused my sister to go to the extreme — to the point where my wife and

I left and spent the night at a hotel because we didn't know what she might do next. It was a terrible moment, because my wife had never seen that side of her. But since that incident, my wife has understood the relationship I have with my sister. My wife has been a big help and a huge support in helping me to love and encourage my sister, to be understanding, and to set boundaries along with learning to be patient and loving as I set boundaries with my sister.

The most important lesson I've learned and continue to learn is no matter how many times a person hurts you —forgive, forgive, forgive and love, even when it is hard to love that person, and you feel you've repeatedly been done wrong. It is tough for people to do that. It is tough for me to do that. There have been times when I wanted to get back at my sister, to rough her up for causing my mom and I heartache.

One thing was for certain — my sister would not come at our father like that. My dad was not afraid to put my sister in her place. As I reflect on it, even though brothers and sisters are raised in the same family, they can turn out differently. The impact of the things my dad did affected my sister in a whole different way from the way they affected me. My sister was affected in a way that made her take things out on me and my mom. Meanwhile, I held things in, and I wanted to leave home to experience a new life and be around new and different people. I wanted to find my own way in life and carve out my own path.

Sometimes I ask myself, what if I had never left home? What would have become of me? What would have become of the path I've been on? I've come to believe I was meant to leave the place where I was raised. My relationship with my dad and my sister — they were part of the process of this journey I am on. They were some of the steep hills in my life.

As a young boy, or even a young man, I was not taught to be vulnerable, to be open and share my feelings. I believe leaving home is what I needed to find my true self; to go through the process of life and help me relate to others. It strengthened me in dealing with my sister, and taught me to be patient, to listen, to let her talk, to stay calm, to step back, and to be slow to speak as in "*James 1:19. Everyone should be quick to listen, slow to speak and slow to become angry.*"

I learned over the years to develop a spiritual mindset because of my relationship with my Heavenly Father. I learned that my sister needed help; it was a mental thing. She has since gotten help for what we now realize is a bipolar condition — a mental sickness that could have been caused because of our relationship with our earthly father. We really don't know. Now that I understand her condition, when I want to get upset or angry with my sister, I have to remember that is not her fault.

No matter what struggles I have with my sister, she means well, and she does love me and cherishes the time we have together. Even though I am younger, she sometimes looks to me for support. Sometimes I jokingly give her a hard time.

I appreciate her excitement when she knows I'll be coming out to South Carolina to visit, and she wants to hang out with little brother and sister-in-law. I can't take these moments for granted, knowing that life is short and fragile, and nothing is guaranteed.

I may not have a perfect relationship with everyone. But I do know my Heavenly Father put the right people in my life at the right time. That doesn't mean my experiences with those people will feel good. But they can teach me to be a better person, to love unconditionally and forgive no matter what. My relationship with my sister is a test of my faith. I love her and I want the best for her, but our relationship is, and probably always will be, a work in progress, especially for me, as I continue to learn to be a better person.

CHAPTER THREE

The Love of Mom

Even the greatest humans who ever lived were not perfect. We have all made mistakes here and there, except for Jesus Christ, in my belief. But when it comes to perfect love, my mother's love was almost that. I made many mistakes growing up, but the love of a mom trumped all of them. The one comfort I could count on in my childhood was her love, and even as an adult, my mom's love came through in my darkest times, when I needed it the most.

She sacrificed a lot for my sister and me. She worked hard as a seamstress at a sewing plant for most of her adult life, earning minimum wage, which was about $3.80 per hour. She worked as much overtime as she could to give us what we needed, not always what we wanted.

I still remember one of my most embarrassing moments as a young kid, which took place when I was in fourth or fifth grade. I was in class, and the teacher had stepped outside in the hall. All of the sudden I had to use the restroom really bad, and I was afraid to say anything — so I peed on myself. As I think about that moment some more, I realize I had great classmates, because they never made fun of me or even brought the situation up. I was in denial. The school called Mom, and she left work and brought me a change of clothes. She didn't yell at me or spank me. That was the love of a mom and the love of my classmates. That incident was never brought up again, at least in front of me.

Even as a young adult, when I ran out of money over and over, just from being irresponsible, my mom would sacrifice the last of what she had— and she did not have a lot, making minimum wage. I would call her, and she'd send me $20 in the mail. That doesn't seem like much now, but it was plenty back in the '90s. When I got my first full-time job in Charlotte, I didn't have a car to drive back and forth from work. My mom sacrificed again: She gave up her car so I could have a way to get around. Charlotte is three or four hours from my hometown. To give up her transportation for me to get to work, she had to depend on others so that I didn't have to struggle — that shows love, the love of a mom.

One of the toughest periods in my life was the time I spent in Atlanta. I was locked up in the DeKalb County Jail for three weeks — that's another story in and of itself, which I will get to later. The first night I got out, I sat alone in a dark room in my apartment, and the first thing I did was call my mother. Bawling, I apologized and told her how terrible I felt for getting myself into the mess I was in. My mom's love came through again. She comforted me, and I felt it through the phone with her simple words, "Are you okay?" You will be okay."

A mom's love is knowing that if you go home to visit, and you fall asleep on the couch, she will take a blanket and cover you up whether you're eight years old or twenty-eight years old. That was my mom's love.

All that said, it hurt me to the core to know the pain my mom was going through during her battle with cancer. One of my greatest regrets, if not the greatest, is not spending time with her as she was climbing that hill in her life because of my obligation to the military later on in my life. I have asked myself whether I regret going into the Navy. I don't regret it; I needed the Navy to help me forward in life. It was part of a greater plan.

The last few times I visited her, I knew she was not the same person. She spent most of her last days and weeks lying in bed in pain. I believe my mom try to put up a good front, but it was tough. The cancer and chemo were taking their toll on her, and it was tough to see.

One thing I miss most about my mom is her smile. I would like to say I get my smile from her. I still have a picture of my mom showing her last day of chemotherapy, ringing the bell, and of course she had that smile. Little did she or anyone else know that she would only have a couple more months here on this earth.

The biggest lesson I received from my mom, which I still carry today, is: "Be respectful. Respect will carry you a long way more than money will." Yes, money gives you options, and maybe a little bit more freedom to do things, but respect will open doors that you never, ever would have thought could open for you. Respect will build long-lasting relationships that will help you climb that mountain in life. It has done that for me so far.

When my mother was in hospice, and my father finally relented and told me to come, I caught the earliest plane possible out of San Diego to spend more time with her. It was a tough flight, especially waiting at the airport during layovers. My mind was all over the place. I didn't know what to expect as I prepared to see my mother one final time.

I don't remember who picked me up at the airport and drove me to the hospice center. I just remember going into the room. Seeing her lying there, without knowing whether she was aware that I was there or not, was tough. Her eyes were somewhat open, but she was not able to talk or respond. I told her to hold my finger, and I wanted to believe she did hold my finger and she was aware and happy that I was there with her, but I wasn't sure. She was at a point where she was not able to eat anything. I spent the week playing music for her, talking to her, being in her presence. I wanted to be next to her.

I still remember the last day I spent with her; the day she went to sleep forever. It was Nov. 11, 2011. Veterans Day. It was the day I was hoping to watch my favorite college basketball team, the UNC Tar Heels, play from the deck of aircraft carrier CVN 70 Carl Vinson in San Diego. That was the ship where I spent my four years of active duty; the ship that took me away from spending time with my mom during her sickness. I was obligated to the Navy life.

The Hills We Climb:
Love it, Hate it, Embrace it...Life's Journey

The nurse and caregivers came in to change her, and I stepped out. I went to the cafeteria to grab something to eat and watch some of the basketball games on TV. The nurses came into the cafeteria and gently told me my mother had passed away. Those were words that I did not want to hear. It hurt so much.

I was fortunate to have been able to spend that week with my mother. "God gives and God takes away, Job 1:21." I am blessed that my Heavenly Father gave me a mom who showed me unconditional love, who gave me everything I needed — not everything I wanted — and who sacrificed so much to go without so that I could have. Who worked overtime at her job, who put our clothes on layaway to make sure we had something to wear. Just the simple stuff. Sleeping on her lap during church services. Riding with her and my sister to the laundromat and grocery store on Friday nights. Going to the local ice cream shop before it closed down – she always got strawberry, which was her favorite, or butter pecan. Every time I eat strawberry ice cream, I think about my mom, who gave me her smile, but also taught me to toughen up. The love of a mom--at least the love of *my* mom.

CHAPTER FOUR

The Journey Away from My Family

As much as I love my family, it was so hard staying under the same roof with my dad. Maybe I was Peter Jr. to some people back home — my father's name was Peter, and we did look alike — but in personality, I believe we were not the same. I was truly desperate to leave home.

With the limited options I had when I left high school, I was blessed to have been given the opportunity to attend the Nielsen Electronic Institute (NEI)in Charleston. NEI was a combination school — there were people who went there for electronics and people who went there for truck driving. I went there to study electronics, but mostly I went there to get away from home, to be free, to live my life how I wanted to, somewhat. Along my journey in life, I have often asked myself what I've gotten myself into. Going to that small electronics/truck driving school was one of those moments, but I was not going to turn back.

Before I went to Charleston, I spoke with the school director on the phone to learn more about what the school offered. This was, of course, before we had Zoom, Microsoft Team, or Facetime. The first thing that caught my attention during our talk was his name: James (Jim) Brown. I wondered if he was Black, because both his first and last names were associated with famous African American men. He did a really good job selling the school to me and probably other kids like me. He talked about the school having a basketball team, a dormitory and all of that. He didn't have to con me or work too hard to convince me I was ready to leave to begin this new life journey.

My parents drove me to Charleston. When we reached the school, the first thing that stood out to me was the street the school was located on. It was a rough area, but I got over that. Then Neil, the van driver, led us to the dorm I was going to call home for about two years. As we turned in, I was thrown off — the dorm was actually a trailer park—the kind you find in a low-income neighborhood--with a beat-up basketball court.

Everything the school director had talked about seemed to be far from the truth. I had been bamboozled and hoodwinked. A victim of false advertisement! This was not the vision I had of what the school was going to be like, but I was *not* going back home. I was going to move forward and adapt and adjust to my new life for the first of many times.

I often wonder what went through my parents' minds when they dropped me off at my dorm room, or trailer, rather. Once inside, we met one or two of my roommates and some other fellas who were hanging out there. One dude was drinking alcohol. A couple of other dudes were high — their eyes were red from smoking weed. One of the dudes was high with a machete! That was crazy!

I seriously wondered what I had gotten myself into. I thought my parents had to have noticed what was going on — or maybe they hadn't. I will never know. They said their goodbyes and I was left on my own.

It didn't take long for me to adapt and adjust in life without them. I actually loved being away from home. I was one of the guys, smoking weed and getting drunk over and over. I enjoyed the party life. I was getting turnt up before they invented the phrase "turnt up." After two years at the school, I graduated with a degree in electronics, but I was not good at the craft. I look back on it now and see it was not my calling.

I did develop some meaningful friendships with guys, who really turned into brothers, and have been with me throughout my adult life. That was the most important thing that happened at that school; those friendships helped me to overcome some hills in my life.

The school also opened up an opportunity for me to continue my journey in life. Despite being bamboozled, duped and more, it was a blessing in disguise. I believe it was all part of the process that I had to go through, the journey I was, and am on. And that journey next led me to Charlotte, North Carolina.

CHAPTER FIVE

A Place Close to My Heart

Charlotte — how much I love that city. There, I had disappointments, failures, ups and downs, peaks and lots of valleys. I had a spiritual transformation; I built lifelong friendships. There were lots of hills to climb.

After I graduated from the electronics school in Charleston, a job recruiter visited and helped some of the graduates get jobs in the electronics industry in Charlotte and Atlanta. I was one of those recruited.

After that, it was a waiting game to see what doors would open first. Because of that, I had to go back home. While I was waiting, I decided I needed to work, so I started applying to jobs. I had one interview, but it didn't work out. I imagined it wasn't meant to be.

The Hills We Climb:
Love it, Hate it, Embrace it...Life's Journey

Eventually, I did get the phone call that I was hoping and looking for in 1996. I got the opportunity to work at IBM, aka the Big Blue Machine, which was the place to be at the time. I was thrilled to share the news with my family and friends. I had finally gotten my ticket to leave home and never turned back.

To me, Charlotte was the Big City compared with my hometown. It was a city on the rise; the megacity of the Southeast, looking up to Atlanta. At the time, the IBM brand was known worldwide, and I was thrilled to be working there! I thought I was going to wear a suit and tie every day at work. Nope. I wore a lab coat. I was testing circuit boards.

I had my future all planned out in my head. Work at IBM for twenty years or more, retire from there, and call Charlotte home for good. None of that came close to happening. I guess my God had other plans for my life.

Like I said before, I am grateful for the people that God placed in my life at the right moment and time. When I arrived in Charlotte, I didn't have a car, a driver's license, or a place to stay. I was behind the eight ball. Again, at the right moment, God stepped in. I was able to get my license, and a childhood friend and his girlfriend let me stay at their place. Still, IBM was a good distance from where I was living. With no car, and no knowledge of public transportation, I was at a loss. Then, a mom's love came through again — my mom sacrificed by giving her car to me so that I had a way to get to work.

Eventually, I needed to find my own place to live. I did some apartment hunting and was able to find a place, but there was one obstacle — I was not 21 years of age. I needed a co-signer. A mom's love came through again, and she co-signed for me. But she told me one thing — not to let anyone live with me. She meant I shouldn't let anyone move in with me. It was only a one-bedroom apartment. I was young and dumb, and I did not listen. I was living something of a wild life, and I let one person move in with me, thinking that one person wouldn't hurt anything. Vince was a graduate from the same school

I went to in Charleston. We were roommates also and ended up becoming great friends. Even today we are connected like brothers, and we have reconnected throughout the years (That is another story to tell).Vince has been there for me so many times. God is always putting the right people in my life at the right time.

After Vince moved in with me, the floodgates opened up and more fellas moved in. We all were working at IBM, but different shifts. Imagine the money I could have saved but didn't — I didn't know any better. Things were going OK. I was working at IBM, hanging out with the fellas, having girls over, going out partying, getting "turnt up", getting wasted every chance I got. All of a sudden, there was a layoff at IBM! What the heck?! I had no money saved — shame on me. But I was able to recover. I got another job with a company that bought out IBM, and life was still pretty good.

Transformation

My time in Charlotte was a sort of transformation process. I believe God was calling me or showing me there was a better way of life than the one I was living, and there were better things to do than the things I had been doing.

I grew up going to church and doing all the right things, but starting in my teens, I began living another life. I started out drinking really heavy malt liquor and smoking weed. I wanted to belong with the cool kids-- hang out with the big dawgs, I was trying to fit in and find where I belonged, I guess. I really enjoyed that lifestyle, and it gave me the sense of belonging I was looking for.

In college and then in Charlotte, everything went to a whole other level. I went from 40 ounces of Malt Liquor to beer, gin, vodka, and mixed drinks. There were plenty of times where I just got wasted, torn up, spilling gut, with a bucket right next to my bed, telling myself I would not do this again, and then I was right back at it again, over and over. I also spent time at strip clubs to meet my needs or indulge in sinful pleasures.

I continued in that lifestyle for a few years, and one day I was by myself at a laundromat, minding my own business and washing my clothes, when this lady came out of nowhere and handed me a church card/invite. I believe God was trying to get my attention by putting this lady in my life to reach out to me. I was curious about the church, so I call my "road dawg" and told him about the encounter I had with this woman. We decided to go check out the church, but I wasn't ready to commit. I loved the life I was living.

But soon things started to change for me in ways that were not so good. Sometimes the things you do can come back on you, and maybe God was trying to get my attention. My mother had told me not to let anyone move in with me. But over the years, I had people coming and going from my apartment, and eventually that caught up with me. The landlord found out that I had other people living in my apartment, and just like that, I was kicked out after all those years.

I was really in a deep mess, but I did not want to move back home. Eventually, another good friend who went to the same electronic school and had his own place decided to let me move in with him and his then-girlfriend. He was just like Vince and ended up being a lifelong friend of mine — and the best man at my wedding.

Chance after chance came my way; opportunity after opportunity. But the struggles continued. I had just finished making my last payment on my Ford Tempo when I was involved in an accident that totaled the car. I replaced it with a nice candy-apple-red Pontiac Grand Am. Then, I fell behind on my car payments and my Grand Am was repossessed.

Life was not going so well. Doing the same old clubbing, partying, drunkenness and everything else was starting to get old for me. It was time to surrender my life to something more meaningful. I vaguely remember the last time I stepped into a strip club in Charlotte. I was empty, and it was not fulfilling my needs. I'd had enough.

God needed to put people in my life to guide and direct me in this life, to show me where I needed to be. He used this friend that I was staying with to tell me I needed to go to church — even though that friend wasn't going to any church! I did go back to the same church, but I knew I needed to be fully committed, not halfway in.

The year was 1999. I thought the end of the world was coming because the year 2000 was approaching. It was a new century and a new millennium; almost everyone thought the world was going to end or there would be some kind of apocalypse. However, I survived Y2K and started a new chapter and a spiritual transformation that would start my new journey.

New Relationships, New Journey: More Hills to Climb

Charlotte was the city I grew up in, and it was where my spiritual transformation happened. I gave up going to the strip clubs, getting drunk and smoking weed, but still I had my struggles. There was constant temptation to go back to that lifestyle. There were still plenty of hills to climb, and I was still trying to find my way, to find out who I was and where I belonged. I was able to establish meaningful friendships and relationships with people inside and outside the church, which I still have today, more than twenty years later. I learned a lot from so many people.

In Charlotte, the people were good to me, and I have so many good memories. I have been helped in so many ways. It's always a joy to go back and visit the Queen City and go down memory lane. Despite the disappointments, and the things that didn't pan out like I'd hoped, I gained relationships with people that would last a lifetime, and memories that I hope I never forget. I have nothing but love and gratitude for the city, and the people. Charlotte will always have a place in my heart and my life, but there are other places and memories I'd rather forget.

A City of Regret; a Moment to Forget

Sometimes in life we have moments we want to forget about. Maybe you have a regret, or you wish you could have done something differently. Have a do-over. That's not possible. But what *is* possible is to learn from those moments. That was the situation during my time in Atlanta.

I moved to Atlanta from Charlotte because, as much as I had enjoyed living in Charlotte, I felt it was time to move on. My goal was to go to mortuary school and go into the funeral business like my grandfather. But no matter what I tried, none of my plans worked out. In fact, my time in the ATL was one of the toughest hills I ever had to climb. Maybe going there was a mistake;

maybe I could have waited and planned things better. Maybe it wasn't the wisest decision — or maybe my God had a lesson for me to learn.

When people say the impossible is possible, they usually mean it in a good way. My time in ATL, though, was not so good. If not for the brothers in church and my former co-workers, I don't know how I would have made it through my time there. From having my car stolen, to having to move from place to place, to having an unstable job situation — things did not line up for me. I could not put the blame on anyone else. I put myself in that situation by moving to Atlanta. I didn't prepare or plan it out like I needed to. I was just ready to take the next step in my journey.

I think the toughest time I had was being locked up in DeKalb County jail for three weeks! You might say, okay, three weeks, what is that? But for me, that was too long. Being stopped by the police, being handcuffed, being locked in a holding cell and transferred to county jail, being told to take off my clothes and put on the orange county jail jumpsuit— that was when things got real, and the impossible became possible in a bad way. That moment in time was beyond my wildest imagination. That moment was something I did not want to imagine.

How it happened is a bit difficult to explain. It started out with me driving my roommate's car, with his permission, when he was out of town. One night, I was stopped by the police for making a right turn on red, which was illegal at a particular stoplight in Stone Mountain, Georgia. The funny thing about it was, I had driven past that stoplight all the time, but I guess I wasn't paying attention that night. As the police ran a check on the license plate, they found there was no insurance on the car, which I did not know!

So, the police took the car and drove me back to the house I had left from. Eventually I had to go to court, but I was not arrested. They gave me a ticket and put me on probation. I went on with life and totally forgot about the ticket. During that time, I got my own car and moved to a new location in the Atlanta area. The car was really old, and a rubber piece hung out from the back of the hatchback, blocking my license plate from being read. I didn't think anything of it. It was pure laziness on my part.

One day, I was driving to work, and a police car was behind me. They stopped me because they couldn't read my plate due to that darn rubber piece hanging out from my car. Once they ran my license plate, they found out that I had a warrant for my arrest for an unpaid ticket because of that right turn on red and the car not having insurance! I could not believe it!

I was unable to call anyone, and no one knew where I was. One mistake had led to another mistake, and something that could have been easily fixed had turned into something that was bigger than it needed to be. This was a moment I wanted to forget, but I needed to remember it so I could learn from it. How something so silly and mindless turned into a headache and trouble that I put my own self in, as well as a headache and trouble for everyone else who had tried to get me out of the mess.

Maybe the toughest part of all this was coming out of jail, going back to my apartment, being in the middle of a dark living room, calling my mom and crying, apologizing for what happened. But the love of a mom came through again, making sure I was okay. That was a tough moment; a tough hill to get over and go past. In addition, I almost lost my job due to being locked up. Thanks to a co-worker who stood up for me and persuaded my manager to keep me on, I was able to get my job back. I didn't have transportation, so when I went back to work, my manager picked me up. On the drive there, I was overwhelmed with emotions, and I found myself crying and thanking my manager for not giving up on me even though he had wanted to fire me. I was grateful for that, and for my co-worker.

There were moments during my time in Atlanta where I needed deep, meaningful relationships and they were hard to come by. I was trying to find where I fit in;

even in church, at times, I didn't feel like I belonged. My soul was yearning for people to know me; for belonging. I did end up finding a couple of church brothers who I was able to form lasting relationships with. After church one Sunday morning, we had a meeting of single brothers, and one of the single leaders, who we called Coop, stood up to speak. He was a big, Black man, about 6'4" tall, and he was a lawyer. He had a deep voice, and he spoke loudly. When he talked, everyone paid attention. He led the meeting that day. I don't remember what the meeting was all about, but I know my heart was full of emotion and my soul was crying, I got vulnerable with the brothers and told them I needed them in my life. I needed deep, true relationships. Brotherly, intimate relationship like King David and Jonathan; love with no sexual involvement, just spiritual intimacy.

It was a desperate time for me in the ATL. I was not happy with my career, and I knew I needed a change for the better. I was willing to go anywhere — well, almost anywhere. I was *not* going back home to South Carolina. Even on my worst day, I refused to consider it, and I had some low days. At one point, my dad called me to check in and see how I was doing. I told him I was not working. He told me I needed to come home. My mind was made up, and I was determined to push forward and find a way to make it.

The last place I expected to move to was New Orleans, especially a year after Hurricane Katrina tore up the city. I first visited the city for a wedding a couple of weeks before Hurricane Katrina. I went with three of my church brothers, who were all either in the wedding or invited to the wedding. We had taken the opportunity to do a road trip from Atlanta to New Orleans.

New Orleans was, and still is, a beautiful, lively place full of lovely people who love their city. While we were there for the wedding, we got to hang out with some people from church, and they were so wonderful. I truly enjoyed my time there for those couple of days.

Little did I know, the city would be my home for a little while.

Chance after chance! An opportunity finally came knocking for me to leave Atlanta for something better — kind of. I have learned that when you leave a place to find something better, things don't always go as planned, and the new place is not always better.

I had been so desperate to leave the Great ATL that I was submitting my resume everywhere, every day! I was a man on a mission. When I finally got that call about a job in New Orleans, working in a shipyard, making a decent amount of money (more than I'd ever made before), I jumped at it. In reality, the job was not guaranteed. But nobody had to know that, and it was a chance I was willing to take.

Did I prepare, and create a plan in case things didn't work out? The answer is no! I didn't have a car to make the four-hour drive to New Orleans. I didn't have a place to live, either. Desperate people do desperate things; sometimes without counting the cost, and I was that person. But I was ready to step into the unknown. I packed everything I had, which wasn't much, and got a friend to drive me to the Greyhound Station. Next thing I knew, I was in the Paris of the South.

So, my few years in ATL were not the best, but as I reflect on my time in the ATL, my Heavenly Father didn't let me fall too far. Once again, he put the right people in my life at the right times. No matter how difficult things got, I was protected. I am forever grateful for the people I met, and the relationships I developed. I believe my time in the ATL was a character builder, part of the process in life I had to go through to create my own story. It was another hill to climb. That hill was no joke. Love It, hate It, but embrace it! It's all part of the journey.

CHAPTER SIX

The Love of the City, the Love of the People

Looking back, maybe jumping onto a Greyhound and heading to a new city wasn't the wisest decision. Or maybe, it was all part of a greater plan beyond my thoughts. But no matter what, I was not turning back again.

Going through Mississippi and Louisiana and seeing the aftermath of Hurricane Katrina, I was in total disbelief. Broken-hearted for the people; the community. One of my goals and desires was to be a help to my church family and the community in New Orleans.

The job in New Orleans was not actually guaranteed, but I was hopeful — or crazy. When I first arrived, I had to live in a camp trailer along with four or five other men for a few days until our job was secure. After that, I lived on a barge on the water with other ship workers until I got an apartment. It was quite the experience.

I jumped at the chance to work at a shipyard on a Naval ship. Who would have thought I'd be living on a Navy ship a year or more later?

Working at the shipyard was more about the money than anything else. It was a good job as an electrician. But I was only good at calling myself an electrician, not being one. That came back to haunt me.

It was a "fake it 'til you make it' situation. I even got a electrical shock one time because I didn't know what I was doing! I wished I had made more of my educational opportunity or paid more attention in my electrician class at vocational school. All the people I worked with *had* to know that I did not know what I was doing; that I was a fraud, a fake, or faking it until I made it.

The Hills We Climb:
Love it, Hate it, Embrace it...Life's Journey

After about a year of surviving in the shipyard, I was let go. I was disappointed, but at the same time, I was kind of relieved to get the pink slip. I did not have a whole lot of opportunities to make the same amount of money — not even close! I ended up at Labor Ready, a New Orleans temp agency, working different jobs, not knowing whether I would even be working day to day.

Once, they had me laying down sod grass on a golf course during summer, The work was tough, the heat was high, and you had to watch out for golf balls coming at you while you were working, At the end of the day, I'd go inside the breakroom and fall flat on the floor; that's how tired I was. Another time, they had me working on a cargo freight barge, which I really did not like either, as it was a dangerous job. Working these jobs and not knowing if I was going to be working day to day was not sustainable. This was not part of the plan but again, no matter how bad it got, going back home to South Carolina was not an option. I was going to continue to climb that hill of life.

As I look back, I see God was setting me up for something else. I was close to my church family in New Orleans, and a certain brother and his friend were Navy recruiters. They spent time telling me that I should join the Navy. One night, this brother actually spoke me joining the Navy into existence. I still remember that moment: he, some other fellas, and I were hanging out playing pool. Afterwards, outside the pool hall, my Navy recruiter friend told me face to face, eye to eye, "You *will* join the Navy!"

In my mind, I laughed at the idea. First, I was already 28 years old. Secondly, I couldn't swim. And third, I hadn't liked my life working in the shipyard. I was terrible at my job. I'd only stayed because the money was good.

But maybe the only opportunity I had left was joining the Navy. I really didn't want to, but it was probably the best thing for me in that situation. Before I decided, I sought advice from my church leader. He advised me that joining the Navy would be good for me.

The Hills We Climb:
Love it, Hate it, Embrace it...Life's Journey

So, I went to the Navy brother and his friend with my decision. It was time, God's time, for me to move on in this journey of life. My church family in New Orleans gave me so much support. My hope in moving to New Orleans, other than work, was that I'd be a help to them after what they had been through with Hurricane Katrina, and what they were still going through. But they gave a lot to me. They supported me through some mistakes I made. Sometimes I felt like I was a burden to my New Orleans Church Family, but I will be forever grateful for them. I was able to build some great relationships with my brothers and sisters in the New Orleans church.

Also, the food experience in New Orleans was one-of-a-kind. I did eat good: po' boy sandwiches, crawfish, baguettes with coffee at the Café Du Monde in the French Quarter. I appreciated the opportunity to learn about the New Orleans culture and what Mardi Gras was truly all about, beyond what we see on TV. It was a family affair where you could bring your kids, your granny and everyone in between to enjoy in the daytime.

Even though I was only in New Orleans for a year, the city and people have a very special place in my heart and life. Going there may not have been the wisest decision. But I have no regrets. I was given another chance at a new start. New Orleans and the Navy were not part of my plan. But they were part of a greater plan and purpose.

CHAPTER SEVEN

What I Got Myself Into

I never thought in my wildest dreams that at the age of thirty-one, my first plane ride somewhere would be to boot camp in Great Lakes, Illinois. Yes, crazy stuff! After some of the recruits and I landed at the airport, we got together with the rest of the recruits and the RDC — the Recruit Division Commander. Wow, it really was happening. We got on the bus, making our way to Great Lakes, which would be home for the next two months — actually, three months for me. On the bus ride, I thought once again, "What did I get myself into?" But there was no turning back now. I often thought about how different things would have been if I'd tried joining the Navy at 18 years of age. Maybe it was just not meant to be.

The Hills We Climb:
Love it, Hate it, Embrace it...Life's Journey

I was the oldest in my division or class of recruits. Someone called me Pops or Grandpops, which didn't offend me in the least. Being in boot camp was a humbling learning experience for me. Since I was older than the others, it might have seemed like I should have led the way for the younger recruits, but it was not in my nature to take control, to be a leader, whether in the Navy or outside of it. I was laid-back and full of self-doubt and uncertainty-- not just in boot camp, but in life. I was afraid to step up, afraid to fail, afraid to embrace who I was as a person.

In boot camp, everything was a mind game. The yelling and screaming did not get to me. I was used to that from my dad. He'd served in the Army, and growing up, he'd treated me like a cadet.

The biggest hill for me to overcome was the swimming test. As a kid, I had attended a swim class one time and that was it. I was terrified of being in the pool, even though there was a swim instructor in with me. As a recruit, I did fail the test. I was disappointed to be unable to take part in the graduation ceremony because I failed. But I did appreciate the love and support of my division, my fellow recruits and my RDC, who rooted for me to succeed. It meant a lot to the old man (me).

Off I went to another division of broken recruits, people who were injured or had other factors that had held them back. While I was in this division, I did come across a few people who were older than me, so I actually did not feel too bad being one of the oldest.

The struggle of the swim test was real; that hill was steep and technical. The whole month of December, I breathed, ate, and lived swimming — that was my life. The smell of chlorine in the pool is still fresh in mind and memory. In the morning, I walked to the swimming pool hall and at night, repeated the same process. I was there so often, one of the trainers gave me the nickname "Crazy Eye" because I had a lazy eye. (I later had eye surgery, thanks to the Navy.) As I think about it, that was not very nice, but I didn't care. My focus, my goal, was to get through the swim test.

I started off in the 3-foot depth, then graduated to the 5-foot. Then to 12-feet off the diving board. I went back and forth, from 5-foot to 12-foot. The Chief Swim Instructor almost gave up on me. I actually doubted whether I could do this or not. Little did I know I had brothers and sisters in the church in New Orleans who were praying for me!

The swim instructors gave me one phone call to make--one lifeline. I was able to talk to Matt, the brother from the church in New Orleans who had convinced me to join the Navy. During our phone conversation, he encouraged me and let me know everyone was praying for me to pass my swim test. I could have given up on my swimming, but that encouragement meant a lot to me. I could have gotten frustrated, tired, weary — but I was going to persevere. There was a higher power at work.

The Hills We Climb:
Love it, Hate it, Embrace it...Life's Journey

I still remember my 12th and last time jumping off the diving board. I was feeling really good that night, maybe because I had prayed before I went out to the swimming pool hall. One of the other recruits was praying for me also. As I climbed up to the diving board, I told myself, "Think happy thoughts." I guess it worked. I was able to float the length of the pool, and the swim instructor in the pool with me confirmed that I had passed the swim qualification. I was full of joy and relief, like a kid in a candy store. It was a big monkey off my back. I also became an inspiration to another RDC at that time, who was watching me, which I did not know. She wanted me to be a part of her division.

It was a special moment; so special that I was able to have a phone call made to the Chief Swim Instructor.

It was during the Christmas holiday and the Chief Swim Instructor was already on his Christmas leave/vacation. He had been on me during the whole time at the swim/pool hall. To pass my swim qualification was a miracle. I was really that bad. He was happy for me. Maybe even surprised. For him to tell me to do good things out on the fleet or in the Navy was encouraging. It meant a lot to have the phone call, just knowing the struggle to get there. After all was said and done, I counted how many times I took that walk to the pool hall — 50 times exactly! I don't know if anyone else besides me went to the pool hall that many times to take the test. I would love to say I hold the record!

Navy Way, Navy Life, New Life in San Diego

I do not know how I made it through my four years of active duty in the U.S. Navy. I did not have a stellar Naval career and still don't as a Navy reservist. But I am grateful for the opportunity that the Navy provided for me, and grateful for the relationships I made and the people I came across who looked out for me. Hopefully, I will be able to help those that come after me.

I was not the best at my Navy job. But I believe I needed to go through the ups and downs of Navy life; they were character builders. I don't think I was ever dedicated to the Navy life or the Navy way. I was, however, full of gratitude for what the Navy did for me. It gave me a stable way of life — a steady paycheck and medical benefits, among other things. I got the opportunity to travel, to experience new things and new ways of life.

Also, it was thanks to the Navy that I had the opportunity to reconnect with a good friend, who was almost like a brother. The way we reconnected seemed like something that could only be written in a book. He was not in the Navy; he was a contractor. One morning, when I was stationed in Kuwait, I was at chow hall for breakfast. As I was walking to one of the tables to sit down, I noticed someone who looked familiar, but I didn't believe that was him. There was just no way, in my mind. So, I went on to sit and eat my breakfast.

I was walking back to my work site after breakfast when I suddenly heard someone calling my name. I turned around and didn't notice anyone. Someone called my name again and again. The third time, I turned around and walked over to see who it was. To my disbelief, I realized it was my friend Vince! I hadn't seen him in at least five or six years, and I would never in my wildest dreams imagined seeing him again in Kuwait! That was one of the most special moments in my Navy career. From that point on, Vince and I have continued to stay in touch and be in each other's lives. I was asked to be part of his wedding in Oct. 2023. It truly will be an honor to be a part of his upcoming wedding party.

The Navy eventually landed me in San Diego. Once again, little did I know, that San Diego would be my home, and would hold the golden opportunity that awaited me. Also, and most importantly, I did not know I would fall in love with a woman from L.A. who lived in San Diego.

My first time in San Diego was a week-long stop in preparation of going to Kuwait for six months. My biggest struggle in the Navy was living up to the Navy standard where my weight was concerned and being able to run a mile and a half during my time on active duty and most of my time in the Navy Reserves. I always had to go through the process of being measured around my waist and neck, and when I was over the weight standard, I struggled to make the cutoff time with my run.

That was another hill that took years to get over. I didn't hate running, I was just not in shape enough for the Navy. I was barely getting by. I had actually had a desire to run, to get in shape, years before I even thought about joining the Navy. It began with the spiritual decision I made in Charlotte to change my life and give up drunkenness, smoking weed, night clubs, and other things.

There was a place in Charlotte called Freedom Park on East Boulevard. At that time, in the early 2000s, it was considered the nice area of Charlotte. There were always people running in the park and around the surrounding neighborhood, and I wanted to be a part of that life and that community. I made the effort for a little while, but I didn't have a strong enough reason to get me to that place. Even during my time in Atlanta, when I had a gym membership, I still didn't know how or wasn't able to have a physical transformation or live a healthy lifestyle.

During my year in New Orleans, just before I joined the Navy, I had a gym membership and I frequently went to a park to run, but I was still not in the best condition. As I reflect again, running was something I always wanted to do. But obstacles prevented me from becoming the runner I needed to be; the food I ate, how much I ate, not having the right people to push me beyond the limits I had set for myself, and not having that wake-up call or light-bulb-going-off-in-the-head moment.

CHAPTER EIGHT

Failing Into Passion

In the Navy, if you fail your physical fitness test, it does not look good on your record. If you fail three consecutive times, you could be processed out of the Navy. I barely met the Navy weight and running test requirements. I was doing enough to get by; to pass. But finally, after years of getting by, everything caught up to me. I ended up failing my weigh-in at 240 pounds.

There were two ways I could deal with this: feel sorry for myself and not do anything to change — or to get over that hill in my life. I chose the second option. Like Michael Jackson said, I was going to make that change. I was determined not to go back to being the person I was before, physically or mentally.

The Hills We Climb:
Love it, Hate it, Embrace it...Life's Journey

To make that change, I needed help; a support system. First, I credit my wife, Carlynn, for holding me accountable with my eating, and the sacrifices she made to help me on the running portion of my life's journey. Then there was the running community. Before I connected with this community, I would run by myself in a park in Bonita called Rohr Park, usually on Saturday mornings.

It just so happened that one Saturday, I came across a group of runners called the Bonita Road Runners (BRR), along with their coach, Tony. The BRR encouraged me to run with them on Saturday mornings, but I was not ready. After three Saturdays, I decided to join them on a run. Boy, I wondered what I got myself into, trying to run with those guys! I was hurting trying to keep up with them — but in my mind and heart, I knew I needed that push to get better, And the biggest thing was, most of them were older than me. So being old was no excuse.

The Hills We Climb:
Love it, Hate it, Embrace it...Life's Journey

On Tuesdays and Thursdays, I was able to go out for morning runs by myself at 6 a.m. Again, I came across Coach Tony and a few other BRR members he was training. Mama Tina Breen, who I am grateful to know, inspired and encouraged me to join them for Tuesday and Thursday morning training sessions. I jumped at the chance.

I learned a lot about running the right way from Coach Tony's leadership and training and the BRR. We did a lot of speed workouts and tons of hill repeats. I learned to embrace the suffer-fest of running, pushing myself to the limits of what I thought I could do. I improved as a runner.

The Marines were another source of inspiration for me. During that time, I had a job working at Camp Pendleton. I was able to go to the gym on the military base and really challenge myself working out with the Marines.

Changing what I ate and how much I ate, combined with running and learning the right way to run, and going to the gym and sticking with it did me a lot of good. I was feeling better and stronger, and was probably in the best shape of my young life. I was transformed physically and mentally, going from 240 pounds to under 200 pounds in about seven months, and from running a 14 and a half-minute mile down to an 11 and a half-minute mile. I've maintained those changes for several years now, and I am still striving to get better.

I also went from failing my Navy weigh-in to becoming a Command Fitness Leader (CFL) at my Navy Reserve Unit. From there I discovered my passion, and eventually my purpose to do more than I ever really thought I could. It was not my plan — this was something bigger at work, something bigger than me.

Passion Into Purpose (6 Years)

I tell people that the best thing that could have happened to me in the Navy was failing that weigh-in.

The Hills We Climb:
Love it, Hate it, Embrace it...Life's Journey

It might sound crazy, but I needed to make the necessary change in finding my purpose, to become boundless in running and in life. In finding my purpose, I was given the opportunity to inspire others with my life, the ups and downs, the obstacles, and hills to overcome. This was about a six-year process.

During those six years, I was able to grow in confidence in the Navy and in life. I had trained to become a medical assistant, and I went back to school to pursue my Bachelors in Gerontology, as I had a strong desire to help the elderly. I received a promotion in my Naval career and was selected as Sailor of the Quarter a couple of times. I ran some marathons and climbed some of the highest peaks in Southern California. I saw the transformation in my life through pushing myself up that hill in running and in life, not giving up.

I fell in love with running and being part of the running community here in the San Diego area. I ran some 5Ks, half marathons, and full marathons, and I attempted one 50k run. The love for running, attacking those hills, getting beat down but coming back again — it's just like life. We have hills — sometimes mountains — to climb, but we find a way to get to the top. All of that ended up being my passion, my purpose.

I also learned to discover the "why" factor; my "why" for running the way I do and persistently climbing that hill. It wasn't only to do better in my Navy career, but also outside the Navy. I knew about my family history of health problems, such as diabetes, high blood pressure, cancer, kidney failure, and obesity. These health issues have also affected my community. Knowing about them has kept me moving.

CHAPTER NINE

My Number One

We all need someone to keep us in check; to keep us honest. A support system. For me, that is my wife Carlynn, my baby girl, my queen. She has supported me from the beginning as I was running races, waking up early to run with my friends, and buying expensive running shoes.

At first, she did not understand why I was doing all this. It has taken her a few years to understand my "why." Our marriage has had our hills to climb. I have put more passion into running than my marriage at times. But she has never given up on me or on us. I needed that gut check to realize I could still enjoy the life of running without neglecting my wife.

The Hills We Climb:
Love it, Hate it, Embrace it...Life's Journey

Carlynn has embraced me for who I am, whether I was running or not running. That is true love. Even before my running journey, my wife supported me while I was getting my career on track, whether I was switching between different jobs or going back to school. Carlynn was the stable one keeping it all together.

I have to say, my wife is the brains behind everything I am doing. Carlynn and I met in a church in San Diego, when I first arrived in the city. I was still on active duty, but we kept in touch while I was deployed. When I returned from deployment, I thought about going back to South Carolina to live, but changed my mind, and my destiny. We got married in 2012, a year after the death of my mother. She and I are on this journey together, the ups and downs, the hills and valleys. She is Mrs. Boundless.

CHAPTER TEN

Being Boundless

I could not have made it this far in life without help from some amazing people who have been placed in my life — those who have helped me become Boundless. "Love It, hate It, embrace It" was and still is my mantra out on my runs, especially going up those hills. Trail running is a "Love it, hate it, embrace it" relationship.

None of that would have happened if Mrs. Erica B Cunningham hadn't been put in my life at the right moment. Usually on our trail runs, we'd talk, laugh, take pictures and shoot videos. One day, Erica was videoing people out on the trails and happened to catch me saying my mantra, "Love it, hate it, embrace It," while running or climbing up a hill. Afterward, she posted it on Facebook.

Seeing myself saying those words put a spark into my heart and inspired me to come up with a crazy idea of turning my passion of running into a business — to be an entrepreneur, selling athletic apparel called Boundless.

My purpose with Boundless is to inspire people like me, who are maybe not the smartest, who struggle with self-doubt, who may think they are too young or too old, or who aren't even the most athletic — but who won't let their age, where they come from, their past mistakes, or setbacks in life put limitations on them. People who won't let those hills in life keep them from reaching the top.

What started with selling Boundless apparel turned into a platform for sharing my story and my life with friends, the running community, co-workers, and family. In 2020, the year of COVID-19, I had the opportunity through social media to share not only my story but also the stories of other people here in San Diego, and eventually other runners from around the world on my "LiveRunBoundless" Youtube Channel. "LiveRunBoundless" has helped me connect with people from different places, and use running as a tool to reach out to people who I might have never met. The past few years have been full of my gratitude for doing the things I am able to do with "LiveRunBoundless", to help people who are willing to be a part of this journey, the people who are inspired from "LiveRunBoundless" and how that encourages me to keep going.

My purpose for "LiveRunBoundless" is to help people embrace where they are right now, but also to embrace the journey that they are going on. To help them continue to climb their hills in life. I want people to take on the challenge of conquering those hills and getting to that certain peak in life, to the top of the hills. You are never too old, it's never too late to set new goals, dream new dreams, try something new ... that is BOUNDLESS.

This Journey

I have been shown a lot of mercy and grace, and I've been given chance after chance and opportunity after opportunity. Lots of doors closed or did not work out, but the right doors opened eventually. I was given the right people at the right time when I most needed them. I did not plan on being on this journey I am on right now. I think of Proverbs 16:9: "A man's heart plans his way but the Lord," my Heavenly Father, has directed my steps.

I am grateful that my God has not given up on me but has shown me what is possible when I decide to step out on faith and put myself out there. To share my journey--to be vulnerable--is hard, but I know it is all worthwhile. What's next on this journey that I am on? Who knows? But I will climb that hill of life and bring other people along with me.

The Hills We Climb:
Love it, Hate it, Embrace it...Life's Journey

My wife and I have tried for years to have a kid of our own, but it has not happened. I have not given up. But we do have a baby great-niece and nephew, so we are a great-uncle and great-aunt. I think about him having to grow up in this crazy world, and I want to leave a legacy for him, to know that his great-uncle has done some great things, that I did not let the challenges of life stop me from moving forward and finding a way to overcome and to do better in life. You don't have to be stuck! You can reinvent yourself. Yes, that is what I've done.

I recently landed a job working at PATH San Diego as an Employment Specialist, which is a great fit for me since I had a lot of different jobs. I help homeless veterans find employment. It really means a lot to me that I am able to serve my fellow veterans, so I am grateful for that opportunity given to me. Even if I did not work for PATH as an employee, I would volunteer my time there; that is how much I truly enjoy working at PATH. It's wonderful to see my fellow veterans succeed and overcome the obstacles along their journey in life, I also appreciate the relationships that I have been able to build with my co-workers. It feels like I was meant for this job, and for this moment. I have seen that what was impossible became possible in my life, little by little, every day; or almost every day. This old country boy from a small town called Hemingway in South Carolina is trying to do something and not giving up. I guess I will have to keep climbing.

There have been a lot of firsts for me in the past year or two, in my career and in running. I completed and crossed the finish line of my first 50k and became an official ultra-trail runner (or baby ultra-trail runner) for the first time. And recently I made my first attempt at running 50 miles! I entered the Ray Miller 50/50 race with a lot of determination. I didn't take a whole lot of pictures. I was so focused on my goal of running fifty miles and the cutoff time at the aid station that I didn't take the time to embrace my surroundings of this epic beatdown course.

The Hills We Climb:
Love it, Hate it, Embrace it...Life's Journey

It was beautiful.

I came up short and did not finish, but lessons were learned!

Respect the mountains and the high elevation.

Respect the training and everything else that comes along with doing this type of racing.

We sometimes have to learn the hard way so we can get better, get stronger, get wiser.

I'm full of gratitude for the ability to put myself out there, test my physical and mental strength, and push through to finish my last few miles. It would not have been possible without the help of some new friends out on the trails — the runners, @keirahenninger, the staff and volunteers, and more specifically, a gentleman we called Skip who led me the last few miles.

CHAPTER ELEVEN

Thankful

Gratitude is a word I have used a lot since I started "LiveRunBoundless". There are so many I owe gratitude to who came before "LiveRunBoundless". My family and my hometown. I love them both. I'm thankful for the love of my mom. I would like to say I have my mom's smile — how I miss her smile, her love, her comfort.

I have gratitude for my dad. We didn't have the best relationship, but I know he loved me the best way he knew how. Because of him, I was determined to move away from home and not look back. Thanks to my sister, through our relationship, I have been able to grow in patience, love and understanding.

The Hills We Climb:
Love it, Hate it, Embrace it...Life's Journey

Thanks to my church brothers and sisters from Charlotte to Atlanta. And the New Orleans church — I only lived in the city a year, but that church has a special place in my heart.

Thank you, Thomas Williams, for being the big brother I needed throughout the years. Ku Le for welcoming me to Atlanta and showing me Stone Mountain on my first day in the ATL with prayer time. The New Orleans Church of Christ, that welcome me in and praying for me.

Thank you, Joe and Joann, Matt and Ashely, and everyone else there who welcomed me with open arms. Thank you, Sister Velma, my spiritual mom who God placed in my life at the right moment to invite me to the Charlotte church.

Thank you to my friends/brothers from NEI: Valentino, Vince, Kenny. Who would have known we'd have been in each other's lives for this long! We had our fun; we grew from boys to men. We started together at

The Hills We Climb:
Love it, Hate it, Embrace it...Life's Journey

18 years old, we went our separate ways, and then we got back together.

I have gratitude for the relationships I was able to develop in the Navy, and the people I came across. Logan, thank you for being a friend. To the San Diego running family: YMCA South Bay trail running group, Coach Tony, Abe, Mama Tina and the BRR/Jedi, Ultrabuds, San Diego Trail Running Crew, Sixrun9, and 5150 Early Morning Running crew; nothing but love.

And I can't forget about the Perros Bravo, BMR San Diego, and Go Be More.

Thank you, Jon Rankin, for being a go-to person before I got started with "LiveRunBoundless" — you inspired me. Thank you for taking the time to talk to me. C.T. (Ms. Connecticut), you went from being my supervisor to being a main supporter in "LiveRunBoundless" (LRB), and I am grateful that our paths crossed again. Thank you to my brothers and sisters in the San Diego Church: Ray and Deshonda, for your support, JD and Debbie for being one of the first to purchase my apparel and sticking with me to support me all the way, and Sandra Eller for coming to San Diego, joining the running crew, and taking the ball and running with it.

Thanks to my Aunt Carolyn, for her support of me, in writing this book and sharing my story. Thanks to my former co-workers who allowed me to inspire them with my life. Thanks to so many people who supported me on my journey and the hills I had to climb in life.

Thank you to Emily Hawgood for believing in "LiveRunBoundless"

Thank you to my "LiveRunBoundless" video editors who put in the work to make me look good, Regina Fernando, Deltamedia and Tyler Maulin. Maggie Guterl aka Maggatronruns,

Thank you to my sponsors/partnerships, who were willing to take a chance on the vision of LRB and allow me to be me:

The Hills We Climb:
Love it, Hate it, Embrace it...Life's Journey

Tailwind Nutrition, SaltSticks, and Rowdy Bar. Thank you to the people I have interviewed and was able to connect with through running.

Thank you to the shoe brand HOKA for giving me the opportunity to be a HOKA Flyer/Ambassador, looking to do some specials things in the community. Also, thanks to Al for being my video guy when I needed to do LiveRunBoundless in-person interviews.

Ms. Kyra, thank you for helping me get my thoughts out, to share my story. Also, another shout out to my Retired Senior Chief Tiffany Ingramm, she plays a important part in my "LiveRunBoundless" from connecting me with a professor Mr. Frank Marshall and his class at Point Loma. I was scheduled to meet with the class around March 17, 2020 and brainstorm ideas for "LiveRunBoundless" but due to COVID never gotten the opportunity to meet the class. Professor Marshall did email a list of ideas that the Class had written down and I still read it and see how far I come from the ideas they had for "LiveRunBoundless" and how the ideas became reality so far.

Thanks to, LT Shonte James, her support of me in my Navy Reserve career and her encouragement in my pursuing "LiveRunBoundless".

Thank you, Erimes Grimes for being a support for me in stepping out and reinventing myself.

Also, I must thank Santa Mujeres Running Crew led by Virgina Lucia Camacho and Priscilla Rojas, co-founders of the Santa Mujeres. They are a female led run crew but they welcome all. In the short amount time they've been around, from the onset of COVID into now, they have made a big impact in San Diego running community and outside of San Diego, as well as outside of California. So much thanks to them for welcoming "LiveRunBoundless" into their run crew. They are a family.

As I was hiking recently, I thought about the path I have been on with my Navy career. I have served for 14 years, 11 currently in the Navy Reserve. I'm at a crossroads, deciding whether to stay in or get out. A wise man seeks advice, and I did that. Yes, I'm only four years away from retirement. Yes, it makes sense to finish out the four years and retire but the decision has not been easy for me. At the end, I just want to do the right thing. Since "LiveRunBoundless" was created and born, and I know I have a bigger purpose beyond the Navy, beyond just me running. What is God telling me to do? To go by faith or go for security and take the safe bet?

One person has truly understood what I've been going through in making this decision. and has been a big mentor to me — Lt. James, an officer and good friend in the Navy Reserve. She explained to me what faith is in her own words and I think it defines my life, my story, and really, everyone's life and story, "Stepping out in faith is trusting God even when you cannot see the blessings that are in store for you. Different people are placed in our path throughout our journey to help us along the way. Ultimately you must trust God and pray, and you will have to decide on what you want to do. What is in your heart?"

I don't know what the answer is yet. But I do know this: whatever I decide to do, and wherever life takes me, I will love it, hate It, embrace It — The Journey.

ABOUT THE AUTHOR

I am a person who spent his whole life seeking and searching where I belong in this world, finding what it is I am good at, what I am passionate about, what drives me… my purpose.

Born and raised in Hemingway, South Carolina, I moved to Charlotte, North Carolina in hopes of living and working in the same city until retirement. I lived in Atlanta, Georgia for a few years, looking for a new start.

I took a chance, moving to yet another new city out of desperation and uncertainties.

I went to New Orleans, LA in hopes of a better life by working in a shipyard. From there, unexpectedly at the age of 31, I joined the US Navy. In my four years of active duty, I was stationed in Virginia and San Diego, CA. I went into the Navy Reserve where I met my wife and discovered the love of running and the desire to run long distances and downhill trail running.

In 2014, I completed my first trail marathon. I attempted a few 50ks (31 miles), and 50-mile runs. I also enjoy every opportunity I get to volunteer at different race events like the San Diego 100 and support my fellow runners.

Currently, I work at a non-profit, serving my fellow veterans. I am a Youtuber and Podcaster with LiveRunBoundless, using running as a platform and a tool to connect with people, to serve people, to share my story and the stories of others in hopes that people will be inspired and encouraged.

Most importantly, I am a man of God who has strived and fallen short but continues to live out my best life in an endeavor to glorify my Heavenly Father.

Printed in the USA
CPSIA information can be obtained
at www.ICGtesting.com
LVHW070424020823
754118LV00018B/355

THE HILLS WE CLIMB

Love it. Hate it. Embrace it... Life's Journey

When you see someone standing on top of a hill or mountain, proud, euphoric and full of energy, you rarely consider all of the times they may have considered stopping, how they had to talk themselves into taking one more step or having to dig deeper than they even knew they went to find the answer to why they chose to scale the mountain in the first place. Yet without those moments, reaching the top of the hill wouldn't mean as much.

Kenneth Pinckney, a motivational runner who has touched athletes and nonathlete hearts alike worldwide, has written an inspiring memoir sharing his life's journey and the paramount moments that forced him to let go of weighty baggage, conquer his fears, and develop new ways to encourage himself.

Rarely do people lay their lives out in front of you in such a vulnerable and transparent way, but then how can you truly understand a victory unless you know where the battle began?

Mr. Pinckney illustrates how the hills we climb in life can be embraced and used to aid us toward conquering our struggles; rejected and walked away from for our own health, or given a special place in our heart as we head for yet another, bigger hill all in an endeavor to become boundless.

ISBN 978-1-958356-22-7

90000

9 781958 356227